The Life of Plants

Claire Llewellyn

W

FRANKLIN WATTS
LONDON • SYDNEY

This edition 2009

Franklin Watts
338 Euston Road
London NW1 3BH

Franklin Watts Australia
Hachette Children's Books
Level 17/207 Kent Street
Sydney NSW 2000

Text copyright © Claire Llewellyn 2006
Concept and design © Franklin Watts 2006

Editor: Jennifer Schofield
Art director: Jonathan Hair
Consultant: Caroline Boisset
Design: Susi Martin
Picture researcher: Diana Morris
Photography: Ray Moller, unless otherwise acknowledged
Artwork: Ian Thompson

Acknowledgements:
Jan van Arkel/Holt Studios/FLPA: 27tr. Andrew Brown/Ecoscene: front cover, 10.
Farrell Grehan/Corbis: 25. Angela Hampton/Ecoscene: 13. Holt Studios/FLPA: 6,
7, 8, 11, 15tl, 19, 21, 22, 23, 24, 26, 27c, 29cr, 29bl, 29br. Eva Messler/Ecoscene:
14. Tony Page/Ecoscene: 12. David Wooton Photographery/Ecoscene: 16. Watts
Publishing : 29cl.

Every attempt has been made to clear copyright.
Should there be any inadvertent omission please
apply to the publisher for rectification.

A CIP catalogue record for this book
is available from the British Library.

ISBN 978 0 7496 9009 0

Dewey Classification: 580

Printed in China

Franklin Watts is a division of Hachette Children's Books,
an Hachette Livre UK company.
www.hachette.co.uk

Contents

What are plants? 6

The parts of a plant 8

Making food 10

What plants need 12

Where plants grow 14

A seed sprouts 16

The plant flowers 18

Making seeds 20

The seeds spread 22

Ways to reproduce 24

Through the seasons 26

Glossary 28

Websites 29

Answers to "What's this?" 29

Index 30

What are plants?

There are many thousands of plants and they live and grow almost everywhere on Earth. Although they are many different types, most plants are green and have roots, stems and leaves.

Plants are alive

Plants are alive, like animals, and share the same characteristics as all living things: they need food to grow; they sense and react to the world around them; they produce young; and they eventually die. However, there is one big difference between animals and plants: animals have to find their food, while plants are able to make it for themselves. They are the only living things that can.

Primroses and celandines are flowering plants with large, conspicuous flowers. Other flowering plants, such as grasses and some trees, have flowers that can hardly be seen.

Try this!

Find an unfamiliar plant, and look it up in a field guide. Field guides group plants in helpful ways so that we can easily identify them. What is the name of your plant?

Plants are old

Plants are the oldest form of life. They have lived on Earth for about 420 million years and, during this time, they have evolved, or developed, into a huge and diverse group. For example, there is not just a single species of oak tree; there are about 800 different species, and each one is unique. Scientists have not yet identified every plant in the world, but they estimate that there are probably about 400,000 different kinds.

Plant groups

In order to study plants, scientists sort them into different groups. One group contains flowering plants, such as oak trees, buttercups, grasses and reeds. Another group contains non-flowering plants, such as seaweeds, mosses, conifers and ferns. This book looks mainly at flowering plants and examines different aspects of their lives.

Ferns grow in shady, often damp, places. Along with mosses and conifers, they do not produce flowers. About one-fifth of Earth's plants are non-flowering.

The parts of a plant

Plants are made up of many different parts. Each part of the plant has its own specific job to do and, by working with all the other parts, helps the plant to live and grow.

Look at a plant

Most plants are made up of similar parts. They have a system of roots below the ground and a stem and leaves above. Some plants have thick roots that grow deep into the ground; others have roots that are fine and widespreading. Some plants have green, soft stems; other stems are brown and woody. Many plants also grow buds and flowers.

Differences in plants

Not all plants have the same parts. Some have adapted to suit the place where they grow (see pages 14–15). For example, some desert plants have spines instead of leaves so that they do not wilt in the heat.

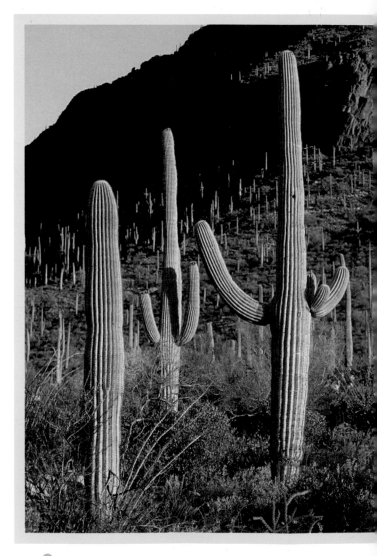

Plants lose water through their leaves so the saguaro cactus – which grows in the deserts of America – has adapted to survive without them.

What's this?

This plant has a woody stem and dark green, very prickly leaves. It has bright red berries and is often used as a Christmas decoration.

THE POPPY PLANT

Every part of the poppy has a job to do. In order for the plant to grow well, each part needs to be strong and healthy.

Flower
The flower produces seeds. Poppies, like many flowers, have colourful petals.

Stem
The stem holds the plant up to the light. Inside are tiny tubes which carry water and nutrients from the roots to other parts of the plant.

Flower bud
The bud protects a new flower. Green leaves, called sepals, cover the bud and open when the flower is ready to grow.

Leaves
The leaves are flat, green surfaces that soak up sunlight and make food for the plant (see page 11). Tiny tubes inside the leaves carry food to other parts of the plant.

Roots
The roots grow down into the ground to anchor the plant. Tiny hairs suck up water and nutrients, which the plant needs to grow well.

Try this!

See how water moves inside a plant. Put some celery stalks (stems) in a jar of water dyed with food colouring. What happens after a few hours? Now cut through one of the stalks. What can you see?

Making food

Plants can make food for themselves. Unlike animals, which have to look for food, plants make it inside their leaves. They do this by using sunlight, air and water in a process called photosynthesis.

Photosynthesis

Imagine that you are hungry. Instead of looking for some food to eat, you go outside and stand in the daylight, and soon feel completely full. This is what it is like to be a plant. A plant's leaves use energy from the Sun, water from the soil, and a gas called carbon dioxide from the air, to make starchy substances called carbohydrates.

What's this?

This small plant stores food in its small, pink and white roots. The crisp roots are often used in salads and taste quite hot.

During photosynthesis, plants give off oxygen, which all animals need to survive. A beech tree produces enough oxygen for ten people to survive on every year.

THE PROCESS OF PHOTOSYNTHESIS

Leaves soak up sunlight. Carbon dioxide enters the leaves from the air.

Oxygen, a waste product of photosynthesis, is given off into the air.

Water and carbon dioxide mix in the leaves to produce carbohydrates.

Water moves up the stem to the leaves.

Water and nutrients are taken in by the roots.

Try this!

Light is so important for plants that they grow towards it. Sow some cress seeds in two small containers. Put one on a windowsill and one in a box with a hole in the side. Put a lid on the second box. What happens after a week?

What happens to the carbohydrates?

The carbohydrates travel from the leaves along tiny tubes to every part of the plant. They give the plant energy to live and to grow new stems, leaves, roots and buds. Sometimes, food is stored in the plant to be used at a later date. The carrot plant stores food inside its root. We eat the roots as vegetables, and they taste deliciously sweet.

A carrot plant stores the food it makes in its orange swollen root. Other plants that do this include parsnips and turnips.

What plants need

Plants have simple needs. They require sunlight, water, warmth and nutrients from the soil.
If a plant lacks or has too much of any of these, it will not survive.

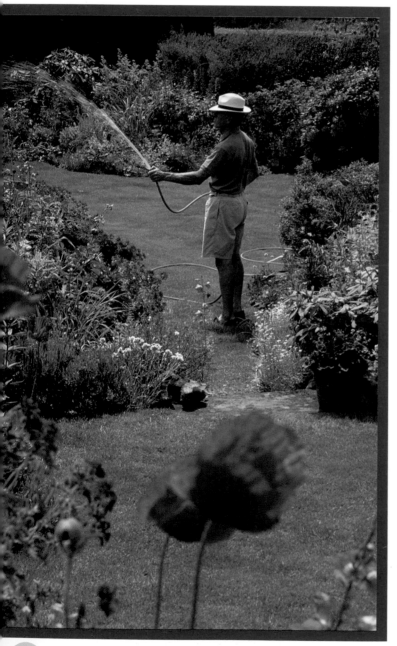

Plants need light

Plants need light for photosynthesis (see pages 10–11). If plants do not get light, they cannot make food for themselves and they starve to death. They start to show this by becoming spindly and pale. Most plants recover quickly when they are brought back into the light.

Plants need water

Water is very important for plants. They take in water through their roots and give it out through their leaves. Many plants cannot survive without water, even for a few days. This is why, for farmers around the world, droughts can be so serious. Some plants, such as cacti, can live on very little water, but no plant can survive with no water at all.

When the weather is dry, many gardeners water their plants to ensure they are healthy and continue to grow.

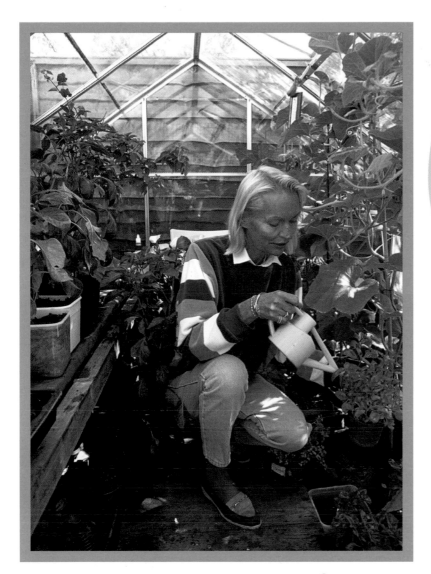

Plants in a greenhouse have lots of warmth and light. As a result, they grow very quickly and need lots of water and nutrients, too.

Get this!

On a warm, windy day, the roots of a large tree can take in 2,000 litres of water – the same amount of liquid as in 6,000 drink cans.

Plants need warmth

Warmth helps plants to grow. It encourages seeds to sprout and speeds up the growing process. In temperate parts of the world, plants grow best in the summer months. They also grow well in greenhouses where they get extra warmth and light.

Try this!

Take two identical healthy plants and put them on a bright windowsill. Water one regularly but do not water the other one. Compare the plants after two weeks.

Plants need nutrients

Although plants can make food for themselves, they also need nutrients that are found in the soil. These nutrients are natural substances called minerals, and are needed only in tiny amounts. On farmland, where crops grow closely together, the minerals in the soil may become used up. Farmers add fertilisers, which are rich in nutrients, to achieve the best possible growth.

Where plants grow

Plants grow in all sorts of places – from marshes and mountains to deserts and the sea – but most plants are suited to a particular place. This is called their habitat.

Adapting to water

Plants have evolved over thousands of years to become suited to a habitat. Those that live in water, for example, have developed ways of keeping their leaves in the light so that they can photosynthesise. Duckweed is a tiny plant that floats on ponds. Its roots have adapted to taking nutrients from the water instead of from the soil. A water lily has also adapted to water. Its leaves have become large and flat – perfect for floating on the surface, where they can absorb plenty of light.

What's this?

This wild flower grows in well-drained, sunny fields, and is often seen around the edges of a crop. It has a simple, bright red flower.

Some plants grow on the banks of rivers and ponds. Others grow in the water. They spread their leaves on the surface, where they can get plenty of sunlight.

The welwitschia grows in the Namib Desert near Africa's south-western coast. Its long leaves take in water from the fog that rolls in off the sea at night.

Try this?

Next time you are in a garden centre, look at the labels on some of the plants. They contain information about the kind of place each plant likes to grow.

WANDA

PRIMROSE
Primula x helenae

PART SHADE

Adapting to drought

Some plants can live in the desert and have adapted to survive on very little water. For example, a cactus has a huge network of roots close to the surface of the ground. This helps the plant to catch water over a wide area during the rare desert rains. Its stem can swell up to store the water.

Adapting to mountains

Some plants have adapted to the high mountains where it is windy and cold. Plants such as the edelweiss have furry leaves and flowers that help to lock in the Sun's heat. Many mountain plants grow low to the ground to keep out of the wind. A few plants even make their own antifreeze to protect them from frost.

A seed sprouts

New plants grow from seeds. Each seed contains a miniature plant. When the growing conditions are right, the seed splits open and the plant begins to grow. This is known as germination.

Life as a seed

Seeds contain two important things: a tiny plant called an embryo, and some food to help it to grow. Most seeds are produced by the parent plant at the end of the growing season. This is not the best time for seeds to grow. Soon, the weather may be too cold for the young plants to survive. So most seeds wait until conditions improve before they germinate. This is often at the beginning of the next growing season, when the air gets warmer and the soil becomes moist and the days become longer.

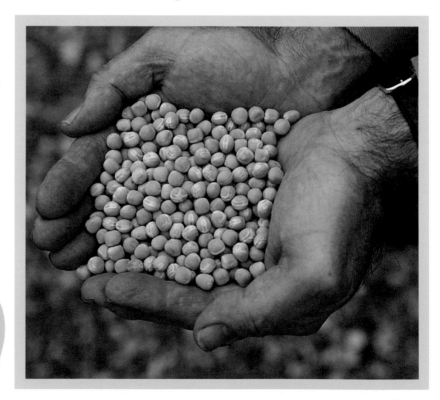

These seeds were produced by pea plants. They can survive until the next growing season because they are so dry. When they are planted, they will take in water and begin to grow.

Get this!

Seeds can survive for many years. Some seeds found frozen in the Arctic were about 10,000 years old. When they were warmed and watered, they began to sprout!

Germination

Most seeds are very dry. Their dryness stops them from rotting and helps them to survive. When the conditions are right, a seed takes in water and oxygen through its skin. The seed swells and the embryo begins to grow, making use of the food supply. The seed splits open and a tiny root appears, which quickly grows down into the soil and begins to suck up water. The dry seed is now a tiny plant. This process of a seed sprouting is known as germination.

Try this!

Discover the best way to grow radish seeds. Try planting them in different ways: deep down in the soil and on the surface; in pots on a windowsill and in the fridge; with and without water. Where do they germinate most quickly?

THE BEAN SEED

The dry seed is planted under the ground. It begins to take in water from the damp soil.

A shoot grows up to the light. The first leaves open and begin to make food for the seedling.

The bean swells and splits. A tiny root grows down.

New leaves grow and the roots extend. The plant grows stronger.

The growing plant

Under the soil, the embryo continues to develop. Using the last of the food inside the seed, a shoot grows up towards the light. The first leaves open and make food for the plant, providing it with the energy it needs to grow new stems and leaves above the ground and longer roots below. The seedling has all the parts it needs to grow and develop into an adult plant.

The plant flowers

Flowers are a very important part of a plant. They are how the plant grows seeds and reproduces. Many flowers are designed to attract animals and so are often bright and scented.

Looking at flowers

Plants grow many different kinds of flowers. Some plants have a single flower. Others have dozens of tiny flowers on a single head. Most flowers develop from buds on the stem. The bud is protected by green sepals, which open when the flower is ready to grow.

Male and female parts

Flowers have male and female parts. These are the parts that make the new seeds. The male parts are small stalks called stamens, which produce a sticky, yellow dust called pollen. The female parts include the stigma and the ovary. Although most flowers have both male and female parts, they cannot make seeds by themselves. The pollen from the stamens of one flower must move to the stigma of another. This process is called pollination.

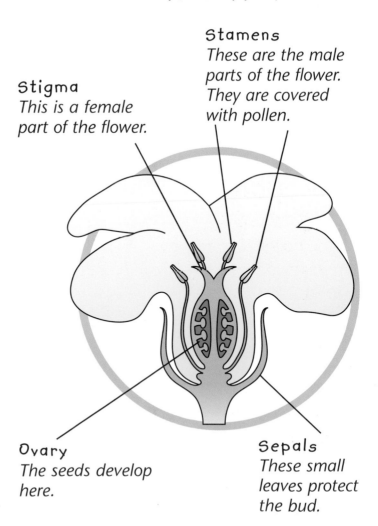

CROSS-SECTION OF A FLOWER

Stamens
These are the male parts of the flower. They are covered with pollen.

Stigma
This is a female part of the flower.

Ovary
The seeds develop here.

Sepals
These small leaves protect the bud.

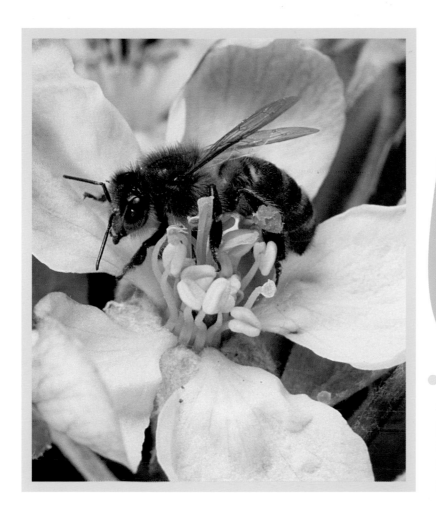

Get this!

A birch tree's pollen is produced by its catkins. On every tree there are thousands of catkins and each one produces more than five million grains. As this pollen is carried on the wind, it makes hayfever sufferers sneeze!

A honeybee gets covered in yellow pollen as it feeds on an apple flower. The pollen will be passed to the next flower it visits.

How pollen is spread

Some pollen is spread by insects and birds. They are attracted by a sweet juice called nectar which is produced by the flower. As an animal feeds on the nectar, pollen sticks to its body. When it feeds at another flower, the pollen from the first flower rubs onto the stigma. Pollen can also be spread by the wind. Many grasses and trees are pollinated in this way.

Try this!

Dissolve some sugar in a little water and pour the syrup into two jam-jar lids. Place the lids on two pieces of card – one yellow, one black – and put them outside, a few metres apart. Which colour attracts visiting insects first?

Making seeds

When a flower has been pollinated, it begins to make seeds. The ovary swells into a fruit, and the seeds inside grow and ripen. This process is called setting seed.

How seeds form

When a pollen grain lands on the stigma of another flower, the flower begins to change. The pollen grain sprouts a long tube. This grows down from the stigma into the ovary, where it fertilises an egg cell called an ovule. Fertilised egg cells grow into seeds. When this process has been completed, we say that the plant has set seed. The ovary swells as the seeds develop, and it becomes a fruit.

What's this?

This tree is very tall. Its colourful candelabra-like flowers make large, brown seeds which grow inside a prickly fruit.

FERTILISATION OF FLOWER

Stigma
Pollen grains land here. Each grain sprouts a tube that growns down into the ovary.

Ovule

Ovary
Inside the ovary, the pollen grains fertilise the ovules and the seeds begin to develop.

The ovules swell
to form seeds.

The petals and
stamens wither.

The fruits grow
bigger.

What is a fruit?

For a scientist, the word 'fruit' has a particular meaning: it is a case that contains and protects a plant's seeds. A fruit may be hard and dry like a nut or green and stringy like a pod, or it may be sweet and juicy like a tomato, peach or plum. Some fruits, such as apricots, contain a single seed. Others, such as poppies, contain a hundred or more.

Pea pods and the flesh of apricots, plums, tomatoes and kiwi fruits protect their seeds.

Try this!

Open a fruit before it is ripe and you will see the developing seeds. They are usually white and moist. They dry out as they ripen.

Get this!

Coniferous trees like pines and firs do not grow flowers. Instead, their seeds grow inside cones.

21

The seeds spread

Seeds spread out in many different ways. Moving away from the parent plant gives seeds the best possible chance of growing into healthy plants.

Scattered by animals

Seeds need to grow away from the parent plant. If they do not, they will be competing with the parent plant, and one another, for water, nutrients and light. Some seeds are scattered by animals. For example, apple and blackberry seeds grow into tasty fruits. When the fruit is eaten by an animal, the seeds pass through its body and are 'planted' in its droppings. Animals also spread seeds such as burrs. These have a prickly surface that sticks to an animal's coat.

Scattered by wind

Many seeds are spread by the wind. Some small seeds, such as thistle and dandelion, have fine hairs that help them float through the air. Larger seeds, like the sycamore or ash, have a kind of wing. This spins them away from the parent plant as they fall to the ground. Tiny seeds, such as the poppy, are shaken from the fruit as it rocks in the wind.

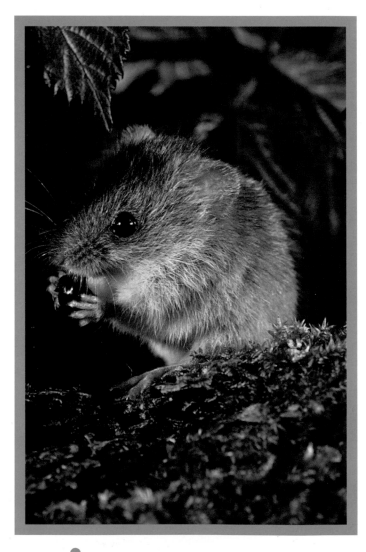

This harvest mouse is eating a juicy berry. The animal will help to disperse the plant's seeds when they pass out in its droppings.

A plant's life cycle

Sometimes, seeds fail to grow – for example, when they are eaten by animals or when they fall on unsuitable ground. Those that succeed, however, follow the same life pattern as the parent plant. First, they germinate and grow. Then, they develop flowers, which are pollinated and fertilised, and set seed. Finally, the ripe seeds are scattered, ready to germinate. These stages in the life of a flowering plant are called its life cycle.

THE LIFE CYCLE OF A POPPY

The plants flower and are pollinated. They set seed.

Young plants grow quickly.

The flowers wither. The fruits grow and the seeds ripen. The seeds are scattered.

Last year's seeds germinate.

Ways to reproduce

Most plants reproduce by making seeds, but some can reproduce in another way, too. New plants can develop from shoots that grow from a plant's stem.

The growing points on potatoes are known as 'eyes'. When the growing conditions are right, the 'eyes' begin to sprout roots and stems and grow into new potato plants.

Try this!

A spider plant puts out long, white runners that grow into tiny plants. Why not try growing one – they are easy to look after?

Underground stems

A new potato plant will grow from a potato, but a potato is not a seed. It is a piece of underground stem, known as a tuber, where the plant stores food for itself. Gardeners dig up potatoes to eat, but if they leave one in the ground it will sprout the following spring and grow into a new plant. Irises also grow from swollen underground stems, called rhizomes. If you break off and plant a piece of stem, it will form a new plant.

Putting out runners

Strawberry plants have a quick way of making new plants. A side-shoot called a runner sprouts from the stem, and grows along the ground. Here and there, new buds grow from the runner and develop into little plants. New roots anchor the plants in the ground. After a few weeks, the runner can be cut and the new plant can grow independently of the parent plant.

How bulbs spread

At the end of the growing season, many gardeners plant bulbs such as daffodils, tulips and hyacinths, to flower the following spring. A bulb is a stem, surrounded by leaves, that contains a supply of food. When the growing conditions are right, the plant uses the stored food to grow more leaves, stalks and roots. Also, buds that lie between the leaves grow into tiny new bulbs. If these bulbs are broken off and planted, they will form new plants.

Tulips grow from bulbs. When the green parts of the plant wither and die, the bulb survives. It will grow again the following year.

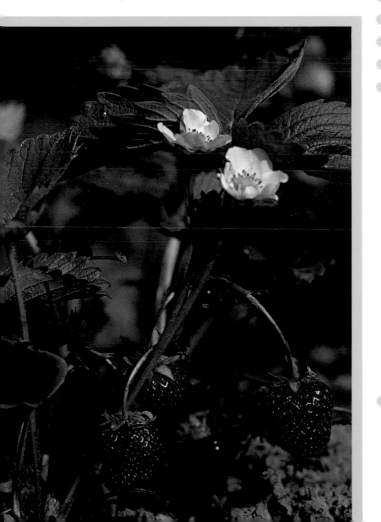

What's this?

This common wild flower is found in meadows. It has a glossy, bright yellow flower and spreads by growing runners over the ground.

Strawberry plants reproduce by putting out runners. These provide new, vigorous plants which produce plenty of fruit.

Through the seasons

In many parts of the world, there are four seasons in the year. Each season brings changes in the light and weather. Plants, such as the apple tree, reflect these seasonal changes in the way they grow.

Spring

In spring, the days get longer and brighter. Stronger sunshine warms the air and spring showers moisten the soil. The apple tree's roots suck up water and nutrients, which rise up inside the tree. Buds burst open and leaves begin to grow. Flower buds also swell and open. The flowers are pollinated by insects and begin to set seed.

It is spring, and new leaves are growing on the tree. The flower buds are swelling and will soon burst open.

Summer

In summer, the Sun is high in the sky and the days are long and warm. The tree is very active now. Its leaves thicken and spread, absorbing sunlight and making food for the tree by the process of photosynthesis. At the base of the old flowers, fruits begin to swell, protecting the seeds that are growing inside. In time, the tree makes buds ready for the following spring.

Autumn

In autumn, the days grow shorter and cooler. On the tree, the fruit continues to ripen and soon falls to the ground. As the light fades, the leaves cannot make enough food for the tree. Its growth begins to slow down. The leaves change colour and begin to dry out. They, too, fall to the ground.

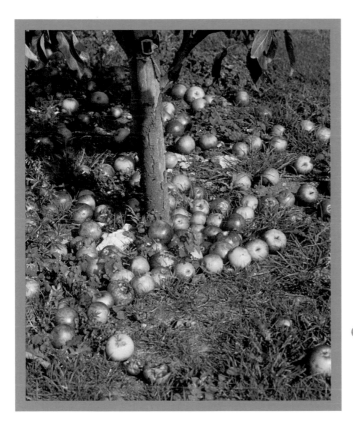

Try this!

Count the number of plant species that grow around your school. Can you suggest places where you could grow some more?

Get this!

Trees grow bigger every year. Each year's growth is recorded in rings inside the trunk. In good growing years, the rings are thick. In poor years they are thin. The number of rings on a tree's stump tells you how old it was when it was cut down.

It is autumn and the ripe fruit has fallen from the tree. Each apple contains a number of seeds, which, if planted, could sprout and grow into new trees.

Winter

In winter, the days are cold and short and the Sun is very low in the sky. Like many plants that grow in the temperate zone, the apple tree's branches are completely bare. The tree stops growing and rests until the spring.

Glossary

Adapt
To change, as a plant does, in order to survive.

Bulb
A short swollen stem surrounded by leaves. Bulbs are the resting stage for daffodils and other flowering plants.

Carbon dioxide
One of the gases in air. Plants take in carbon dioxide during photosynthesis.

Conifers
Mostly evergreen trees that usually grow cones and have needle-shaped leaves.

Embryo
The tiny plant inside a seed.

Germination
The process in which a seed starts to grow.

Habitat
The place to which a plant is best suited and where it usually grows.

Minerals
Natural substances found in the soil. Plants need them to survive.

Nutrient
A substance that gives plants energy and helps them to grow.

Ovary
A female part of a flower, where egg cells (ovules) are stored and fertilised, and the seeds develop.

Oxygen
A gas that is found in air. Plants give out oxygen during photosynthesis.

Photosynthesis
The process by which plants use the energy in sunlight to turn water from the soil and carbon dioxide from the air into carbohydrates, their food.

Pollen
Yellow grains made by the stamens.

Pollination
When pollen is carried from the male parts of one flower to the female parts of another.

Reproduce
To produce offspring. A plant reproduces when it makes new plants.

Runner
A side-shoot that grows from the stem of a plant along the surface of the ground. Plants such as strawberries grow runners.

Seedling
A young plant that has germinated.

Stigma

The tip of the female part of a flower which receives the pollen during pollination.

Stamens

The fine stalks inside a flower that produce pollen. They are the male parts of a flower.

Temperate

A place or climate with moderate temperatures and four seasons in the year.

Websites

www.bbc.co.ukschools/revisewise/science/living/06_act.shtml
This interactive website looks at the different parts of plants.

www.urbanext.uiuc.edu/gpe/
Use your knowledge of plants to help detective LePlant solve a case.

www.copper-tree.ca/garden/index.html
Grow your own plants with useful hints and tips from gardeners.

Answers to "What's this?"

Page 8
Holly

Page 10
Radish

Page 14
Poppy

Page 20
Horse-chestnut tree

Page 25
Buttercup

Index

air 10, 11, 16, 22, 23, 26, 28
algae 7
animals 6, 10, 18, 22, 23, 28
antifreeze 15
apples and apple trees 19, 22, 26, 27
Arctic, the 16
ash tree 22
autumn 23, 27

beans 17
beech tree 10
berries 22
    blackberries 21
birch tree 19
birds 19
branches 27
buds 8, 9, 11, 18, 24, 25, 26
bulbs 25, 28
burrs 22
buttercups 7

cacti 8, 12, 15
California redwood 7
carbohydrate 10, 11
carbon dioxide 10, 11, 28
carrots 11
catkins 19
celery 9
coconut palms 23
compost 23
cones 21, 28
conifers 7, 28
cress 11
crops 13, 14

daffodils 25, 28
dandelions 22
desert 8, 15
droughts 12
duckweed 14

Earth 6, 7
edelweiss 15
eggs 20, 28
embryo 16, 17, 28
energy 10, 11, 17, 28
evolving 7, 14, 28

farmers 12, 13
ferns 7

fertilisation 20, 23, 28
fertilisers 13
field guides 6
flowers 6, 7, 8, 9, 14, 15, 18, 19, 20, 23, 25, 26, 28, 29
food 6, 9, 10, 11, 13, 16, 17, 24, 25, 26, 27, 28
frost 15
fruits 20, 21, 22, 23, 25, 26, 27

gas 10, 28
germination 16, 17, 23, 28, 29
grasses 6, 7, 19
greenhouses 13
growing conditions 6, 16, 25

habitats 14, 28
hayfever 19
honey bees 19
hyacinths 25

insects 19, 26, 28
irises 24

leaves 6, 8, 9, 10, 11, 12, 14, 15, 17, 25, 26, 27, 28
life cycles 23, 28

microscopes 7
minerals 13, 28
mosses 7
mountains 15

nectar 19, 28
nutrients 9, 12, 13, 14, 17, 22, 26, 28
nuts 21

oak trees 7
ovary 18, 20, 21, 28, 29
oxygen 10, 11, 17, 28

parent plants 22, 23, 25
peaches 21
petals 9, 18, 21
photosynthesis 10, 11, 12, 14, 26, 28
plant labels 15
plums 21
pods 21
pollen 18, 19, 28, 29

pollination 18, 20, 23, 26, 28
ponds 14
poppies 9, 21, 22
potato 24

radishes 17
reeds 7
reproduction 18, 24, 29
roots 6, 8, 9, 10, 11, 12, 13, 14, 15, 17, 24, 25, 26
runners 24, 25, 29

saguaro cactus 8
scientists 7, 21
sea 15, 23
seasons 16, 23, 25, 26, 27, 29
seaweeds 7
seedlings 17, 23, 29
seeds 9, 11, 13, 16, 17, 18, 20, 21, 22, 23, 24, 26, 28
    setting seed 20, 23, 26
sepals 9, 18
shoots 17, 24
    side-shoots 25, 29
skin 17
soil 10, 12, 13, 14, 16, 17, 26, 28
spider plant 24
spring 23, 24, 25, 26
stamens 18, 28, 29
stems 6, 8, 9, 11, 15, 17, 18, 24, 25, 28
stigma 18, 19, 20, 29
strawberry plants 24, 25
summer 13, 23, 26
Sun and sunlight 9, 10, 11, 12, 14, 15, 17, 22, 26, 27, 28
sycamore 22

thistles 22
tomatoes 21
tulips 25

vegetables 11

warmth 12, 13, 16, 26
water 9, 10, 11, 12, 13, 14, 15, 16, 17, 19, 22, 26, 28
weather 16, 26
welwitschia 15
wind 13, 15, 19, 22